SPACE

by Anita Loughrey

CONTENTS

INTRODUCTION

Context-based maths gives you a purpose for using maths, and cements your understanding of both why and how maths is applied to daily life. This book explores a range of numeracy skills and topics through 13 different real-life scenarios.

At the head of each section, there's a quick visual guide to the topic and skills covered. The introduction to each section sets the scene and presents the maths question that will be answered.

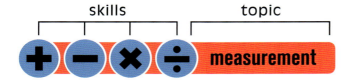

Then you are guided through the process of answering the question, step by step.

In addition, each section also contains helpful tips and an extra challenge: **Now try this** ...

There's an answer key for the **Now try this** ... challenge at the end of the book and words covered in the glossary are highlighted in **bold** throughout the text.

HOW MANY HOURS ARE THERE IN A YEAR ON EARTH?

Your brother has just had his birthday and he already wants to know how long he has to wait until the next one! You tell him there are approximately 365 days in a year — which is the time it takes for Earth to orbit the Sun. He wants to know how many hours this is.

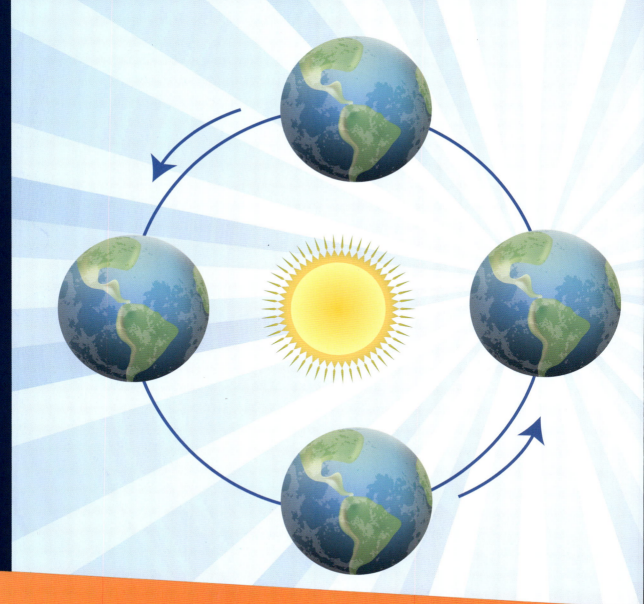

You know there are 24 hours in a day. To work out how many hours there are in 365 days you need to multiply 365 by 24. You can make it easier by partitioning the 24 into 20 and 4.

365×20
365×4

Start with the first number sentence. First, remove the 0 from 20 so you are multiplying 365 by 2.

```
  3  6  5  ×
        2
  7  3  0
     1     1
```

Don't forget to put the 0 back again:

$365 \times 20 = 7300$

Then multiply 365 by 4.

```
  3  6  5  ×
        4
1  4  6  0
   2     2
```

Finally, add your answers together to find the total number of hours in a year.

```
7  3  0  0  +
1  4  6  0
8  7  6  0
```

 There are 8,760 hours in a year – that's how long your brother will have to wait until his next birthday!

Make it easy!

Partition numbers to make it easier.

$24 = 20 + 4$

Simplify calculations by removing 0s first.

365×20

365×2

But remember to put the 0 back on the end of your final answer.

Now try this...

There are **366** days in a **leap year**. How many hours would that be?

HOW DO YOU WRITE THESE NUMBER WORDS AS NUMERALS?

For your school project, you're going to make a space-themed game. Your teacher has given you answers to two of the questions in your game.

The **radius** of Earth is six thousand, three hundred and seventy-one kilometres. The radius of the Moon is one thousand, seven hundred and thirty-seven kilometres. Can you write these numbers in their shorter form, as **numerals**, on your answer cards?

Radius

Radius

When you convert words to numerals, you partition the number into thousands, hundreds, tens and units.

The radius of Earth is six thousand, three hundred and seventy-one kilometres so there are six thousands, three hundreds, seven tens and one unit. You can write the numbers in columns to help you:

Th	H	T	U
6	3	7	1

Don't forget to write a comma after the number in your thousands column. Also, remember to write the unit of measurement that comes after your number that helps to answer the question.

The radius of the Moon is one thousand, seven hundred and thirty-seven kilometres. If you partition the numbers, you have one thousand, seven hundreds, three tens and seven units. Again, write the numbers in columns to help you:

Th	H	T	U
1	7	3	7

And don't forget the comma after the number in your thousands column and the unit of measurement after your number.

The radius of Earth is 6,371 km.
The radius of the Moon is 1,737 km.

Make it easy!

Always include the unit of measurement you are working with in the answer.

mm = millimetres
cm = centimetres
m = metres
km = kilometres

Placing a comma after the **thousands** in **numerals** makes them easier to read:

6,200

Now try this...

The radius of Mars is three thousand, three hundred and ninety-seven kilometres. How do you write this in numerals?

HOW MANY MINUTES DOES SUNLIGHT TAKE TO TRAVEL TO EARTH?

Your friend tells you the light from the Sun takes 500 seconds to travel to Earth. Can you work out how many minutes there are in 500 seconds?

You know there are 60 seconds in 1 minute. To work out how many minutes it takes light to travel from the Sun you need to work out how many 60s there are in 500. **Chunking** can help you calculate quickly:

60 + 60 = 120
60 + 60 + 60 = 180
60 + 60 + 60 + 60 = 240
60 + 60 + 60 + 60 + 60 = 300
60 + 60 + 60 + 60 + 60 + 60 = 360
60 + 60 + 60 + 60 + 60 + 60 + 60 = 420
60 + 60 + 60 + 60 + 60 + 60 + 60 + 60 = 480

So there are 8 minutes in 480 seconds, with 20 seconds left over.

 Light takes 8 minutes and 20 seconds to travel from the Sun to Earth.

Make it easy!

Remove the 0s in **multiplication** and **division sums** to make them easier.

60 × 8

6 × 8 = 48

But don't forget to put them back again . . .

60 × 8 = 480

Look for relationships between numbers. You know there are 60 seconds in 1 minute so you can use your **6 times table** to help you work out the answer.

Now try this...

Light takes 760 seconds to travel from the Sun to Mars. How long is this in minutes?

WHAT ARE THE COUNTDOWN SEQUENCES?

Before a rocket blasts off there is a countdown. The numbers go backwards from 10 to 0. The astronauts are bored of having the same countdown so mission control has come up with some new countdown **sequences**. Some of the numbers have been wiped off the whiteboard. Help the astronauts work out the sequences.

Sequence 1: 17, 16, 15, ___, ___, 12, ___, ___, 9, ___

Sequence 2: ___, ___, ___, 14, ___, ___, ___, 6, ___, ___

Sequence 3: ___, ___, ___, ___, 45, 37, 29, ___, ___, ___,

You can work out number sequences by looking at the difference between **adjacent** numbers.

10
9
8
7
6
5
4
3
2
1
BLAST OFF!

Sequence 1: 17, 16, 15, ___, ___, 12, ___, ___, 9, ___

Look at the relationship between 17, 16 and 15. Each number goes down by 1 each time. Now look at the blank spaces.

To find out the missing numbers, continue counting down in 1s.

Sequence 2: ___, ___, ___, 14, ___, ___, ___, 6, ___, ___

You can see that the numbers are going down again. The numbers are also even numbers. The even numbers between 14 and 6 are 12, 10 and 8. You can see that there are 3 gaps to fill so 12, 10 and 8 must fit there. Now that you know that all the missing numbers are even and go down from left to right, you can work out the rest of the sequence.

Sequence 3: ___, ___, ___, ___, 45, 37, 29, ___, ___, ___

To calculate the difference between the first set of adjacent pairs, you can subtract 37 from 45.

```
  T   U
  ³4  ¹5  –
  3   7
  0   8
```

Or you can count up from 37 until you reach 45.

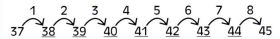

```
   1    2    3    4    5    6    7    8
37   38   39   40   41   42   43   44   45
```

So, it looks like each number in the sequence might go down by 8 each time. Check this by calculating the difference between the next set of adjacent numbers.

```
  T   U
  ²3  ¹7  –
  2   9
  0   8
```

```
29   30   31   32   33   34   35   36   37
   1    2    3    4    5    6    7    8
```

So, there's a difference of 8 between each number. Add 8 to find out the number to the left of a known number. Take away eight to find out the number to the right of a known number.

45 + 8 = 53
53 + 8 = 61
61 + 8 = 69
69 + 8 = 77
29 − 8 = 21
21 − 8 = 13
13 − 8 = 5

Make it easy!

When we **count backwards** the numbers **reduce**:

50, 40, 30, 20, 10

65, 60, 55, 50, 45, 40

Use the **inverse operation** to check your answers:

▪ The **inverse** of **counting backwards** is **counting forwards**

▪ The **inverse** of **subtraction** is **addition**

Now try this...

Look at this sequence of numbers:

___, ___, ___, 26, 15, ___
59, 48,

What are the missing numbers in the sequence?

The new countdown sequences are:
Sequence 1: 17, 16, 15, 14, 13, 12, 11, 10, 9, 8
Sequence 2: 20, 18, 16, 14, 12, 10, 8, 6, 4, 2
Sequence 3: 77, 69, 61, 53, 45, 37, 29, 21, 13, 5

HOW MANY WEEKS ARE THERE IN A MONTH?

Every night the shape of the Moon seems to change as it orbits Earth. The length of a month is based roughly on the time it takes for the Moon to orbit Earth. Months don't have the same amount of days in them but can you work out roughly how many weeks it takes for the Moon to orbit Earth?

There are 30 days in November,

April, June and September.

All the rest have 31,

Except February, it's the only one

To have 28 days clear

And 29 each leap year.

You can create a **table** to show how many days are in each month.

January, March, May, July, August, October, December	February	April, June, September, November
31	28 (for 29 in a leap year)	30

You know there are 7 days in a week. So you can use your knowledge of the 7 times table to help you.

$1 \times 7 = 7$

$2 \times 7 = 14$

$3 \times 7 = 21$

$4 \times 7 = 28$

There are 4 weeks in months containing 31 days, with a remainder of 3 days.

The number of weeks in February is easy to calculate because 28 is in the 7 times table. But, in a leap year, February would have a remainder of one day.

Using the 7 times table again, it's easy to see that there are 4 weeks in months containing 30 days, with a remainder of 2 days.

 There are 4 weeks in each month.

Make it easy!

The 7 **times table** is useful for **calculating** numbers of weeks because there are 7 days in a week.

The **12 times** table is useful for **calculating** numbers of years because there are 12 months in a year.

Now try this...

Most months have extra days that don't make a complete week. Can you work out how many days are left over in a year?

HOW MANY CONSTELLATION SIGHTINGS WERE THERE?

You have just joined the astronomy club and have been looking at different constellations through a telescope. A constellation is a group of stars.

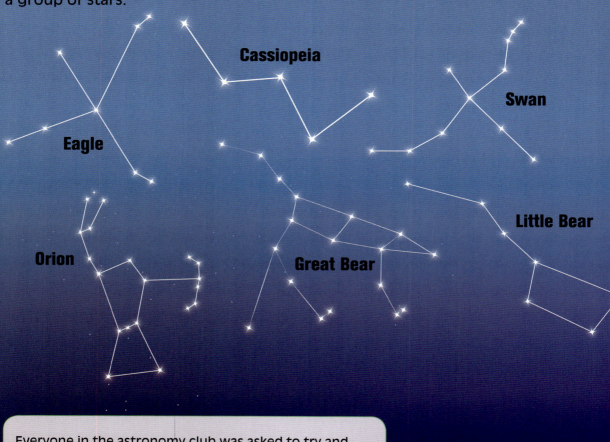

Everyone in the astronomy club was asked to try and find 6 constellations. Some children found all of the constellations and others only found 1. The data was collected and displayed in a **bar chart**. The Great Bear was spotted by everyone, but the Eagle was only spotted by a few children. Can you work out how many more children spotted the Great Bear than the Eagle, and how many constellation sightings there were in total?

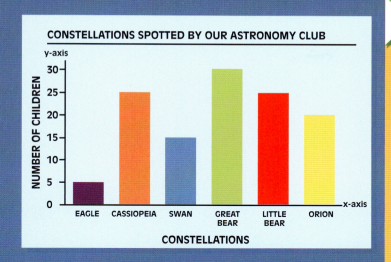

CONSTELLATIONS SPOTTED BY OUR ASTRONOMY CLUB

If you look at the top of the Great Bear column, the scale shows 30. There are 30 children in the astronomy club so this means everyone spotted the Great Bear.

If you look at the top of the Eagle column, the scale shows 5. This means 5 children spotted the Eagle.

To find out how many more children spotted the Great Bear than the Eagle, you need to take 5 away from 30.

30 − 5 = 25

To work out the total number of sightings, you need to read the numbers at the top of each column and add them together. A quick way to add up these numbers is to add up numbers in pairs, starting with the first 2 numbers in the left-hand columns:

5 + 25 = 30
30 + 15 = 45
45 + 30 = 75
75 + 25 = 100
100 + 20 = 120

 25 more children spotted the Great Bear than the Eagle. There were 120 sightings in total.

Make it easy!

The **scale** of a **bar chart** can go up in different **frequencies** to save space and make it easier to read. Always check the **frequency** of the **scale**.

To find out the difference between two numbers, **subtract** the smaller number from the larger number. You can also **count up** from the smaller number to the larger number, using a **number line** to make it easier.

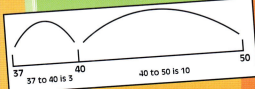

Now try this...

How many more children found Cassiopeia than Orion?

WHAT'S THE BEST TO-SCALE DIAMETER FOR MARS?

You're making a to-scale model of Mars. The **diameter** of Mars is 6,794 km. Can you round this number to find the best to-scale measurement for the diameter of Mars?

**Diameter
6,794 km**

Rounding numbers means adjusting the **digits** up or down to the nearest 10, 100 or 1,000. This will create an **estimate** rather than an exact number.

When you round a number, you need to look at the place value of each of its digits. Place value tells you the value of a digit based on where it sits within a number.

In the numeral 2,222, each 2 has a different value. The 2 on the far right is worth 2. It's in the units column. The 2 to the left of it is worth 20. It's in the tens column. The 2 to the left of that is worth 200. It's in the hundreds column. And the number to the left of that is worth 2,000. It's in the thousands column.

So when you're rounding to the nearest 10, first look at the units column. If the number in the units column is less than (<) 5, the number in the tens column should be rounded down. If the number in the units column is greater than (>) 5, the number in the tens column should be rounded up.

The diameter of Mars is 6,794 km. The number in the units column is 4.

Th	H	T	U
6	7	9	4

4 is less than 5 so it should be rounded down to 0 and the units column should show 0.

So 6,794 to the nearest 10 is 6,790.

When you're rounding to the nearest 100, first look at the tens column. If the number in the tens column is less than (<) 5, all the numbers to the right of the tens column should be rounded down to 0. If it's greater than (>) 5, the number in the hundreds column should be rounded up.

The diameter of Mars is 6,794 km. The number in the tens column is 9.

9 is greater than (>) 5 so the 7 in the hundreds column should be rounded up to 8 and the tens column and units column should both show 0.

So 6,794 to the nearest hundred is 6,800.

When you're rounding to the nearest 1,000, first look at the hundreds column. If the number in the hundreds column is less than (<) 5, all the numbers to the right of the hundreds column should be rounded down to 0. If it's greater than (>) 5, the number in the thousands column should be rounded up.

The diameter of Mars is 6,794 km. The number in the hundreds column is 7.

7 is greater than (>) 5.

So 6,794 to the nearest thousand is 7,000.

Which number is the easiest one to work with on your to-scale model – 6,790, 6,800 or 7,000?

 7,000 is an easy number to work with. It can be scaled down to 7 cm to make your model of Mars.

Make it easy!

If the number is 5 or above, you should **round up** the number to the left.

If the number is 5 or below, you should **round down** the number to the left.

Now try this...

Your friend is making the model for Neptune. Its diameter is 49,527 km. What is this to the nearest 10? What is this to the nearest 100? What is this to the nearest 1,000?

HOW MUCH FOOD DID ASTRONAUTS TAKE TO THE ISS?

You've just watched a programme about life on the International Space Station (ISS). The 4-person crew stayed there for 40 days and ate 3 meals every day. Each food container held 60 meals. Can you work out how many space meals and how many food containers were sent up with them to the ISS.

ASTRONAUT MEALS

First you need to work out how many space meals are required each day. To do this, multiply the number of people in the crew by the number of space meals eaten by one person each day. There were 4 crew members and they each ate 3 meals a day.

4 × 3 = 12

12 meals were eaten by the crew each day.

The mission lasted 40 days so you need to multiply the 12 space meals by 40 days.

12 × 40 =

To make it easier we can remove 0.

12 × 4 = 48

Then we need to put 0 back.

12 × 40 = 480

The astronauts ate a total of 480 meals on the 40-day mission.

To work out how many food containers were sent up into space with the crew, divide the total number of space meals (480) by the amount of meals that fit into one container (60).

480 ÷ 60 =

Remove the 0s to make it easier.

48 ÷ 6 =

You can work this out using the **inverse operation** and your knowledge of the 6 times table.

6 × 8 = 48

Because you are dividing and both numbers had the same amount of 0s at the end, you do not need to put any 0s back in your final answer.

480 ÷ 60 = 8

The astronauts took 480 space meals in 8 food containers on their 40-day trip to the International Space Station.

Make it easy!

Remove the 0 to make it easier. When you're **multiplying**, remember to put the 0 back when you write your final answer. When you're **dividing** if the numbers have the same amount of 0s at the end, you don't need to put them back.

We can check our answers by using the **inverse operation**. The inverse operation of **multiplication** (×) is **division** (÷).

Now try this...

How many containers of space meals are required per person?

HOW MANY TIMES DOES THE ISS ORBIT EARTH EVERY DAY?

From a book in your school library, you have discovered that the ISS orbits Earth once every hour and a half. But how many times does it orbit Earth each day?

You know that there are 24 hours in a day and 1 orbit of Earth takes the ISS 1½ hours. Now you need to work out how many 1½ hours there are in 24. You can do this by dividing 24 hours of time into fractions.

24 hours							
12 hours				12 hours			
6		6		6		6	
3	3	3	3	3	3	3	3
1½ 1½	1½ 1½	1½ 1½	1½ 1½	1½ 1½	1½ 1½	1½ 1½	1½ 1½

A full day is 24 hours.

Half a day is 24 ÷ 2. That's 12 hours.

Quarter of a day is 24 ÷ 4. That's 6 hours.

An eighth of a day is 24 ÷ 8. That's 3 hours.

A sixteenth of a day is 24 ÷ 16. That's 1½ hours.

Make it easy!

We can **divide** time into **equal** parts, or **fractions**, to make it easier.

There are **24 hours** in a day. There are **60 minutes** in an hour.

Now try this...

How many minutes does it take for the ISS to orbit Earth once?

The International Space Station orbits Earth 16 times every day.

HOW LONG DID APOLLO 16 TAKE TO GET TO THE MOON?

Apollo 16 was the fifth mission to land humans on the Moon. It took 4,468 minutes for it to get to the Moon. Can you work out how long this is in days, hours and minutes?

First, you need to work out how many minutes there are in a day. You know there are 60 minutes in an hour and 24 hours in a day.

```
  6 0
  2 4 ×
  2 4 0
1 2 0 0
1 4 4 0
```

So now you know there are 1,440 minutes in a day.

You can use chunking to see how many times 1,440 goes into 4,468.

1 x 1440 = 1440

2 x 1440 = 2880

3 x 1440 = 4320

So 4,320 minutes is equal to 3 days. Now you need to work out how many hours are left over:

```
  4 4 6 8
  4 3 2 0 −
    1 4 8
```

There are 148 minutes left over. You already know that 60 minutes are equal to 1 hour so 120 minutes must be equal to 2 hours.

60 minutes = 1 hour

120 minutes = 2 hours

So 120 minutes is equal to 2 hours. Now you need to work out how many minutes are left over:

```
  1 4 8
  1 2 0 −
    2 8
```

Now put the days, hours and minutes together:

3 days + 2 hours + 28 minutes.

Apollo 16 took 3 days, 2 hours and 28 minutes to get to the Moon.

Make it easy!

Find relationships between numbers.

If 60 minutes = 1 hour

Then 600 minutes = 10 hours

And 120 minutes = 2 hours

So 1,200 minutes = 20 hours

Use **chunking** to see how many times big numbers go into even bigger numbers.

1 × 1440 = 1440

2 × 1440 = 2880

3 × 1440 = 4320

4 × 1440 = 5760

Now try this...

NASA's New Horizons probe holds the record for the fastest ever trip to the Moon. It took 8 hours and 35 minutes to reach the Moon on its way to Pluto. How much quicker was the New Horizons probe than Apollo 16?

WHAT SHAPES CAN YOU SEE IN THE SPACESHIP?

Your sister has found a great picture of a rocket and she wants you to cut out all the different shapes to make a jigsaw puzzle. There are many different types of **quadrilaterals** and **triangles**. Can you give her the correct names for all the shapes?

Quadrilaterals are 4-sided shapes. There are 5 quadrilaterals in the picture. Triangles are 3-sided shapes. There are 4 triangles in the picture. Now let's find out more about these shapes.

The properties of some of the different quadrilaterals have been put into a table. Use the table to help you work out which quadrilaterals you can see in the picture of the rocket.

Name	Image	Sides	Angles	Parallels
Square		4 equal sides	4 right angles	Opposite sides are parallel
Rectangle		Opposite sides are equal	4 right angles	Opposite sides are parallel
Parallelogram		Opposite sides are equal	Opposite angles are equal	Opposite sides are parallel
Isosceles Trapezium		2 sides are equal	2 angles the same	1 set of parallel sides
Rhombus		4 equal sides	Opposite angles are equal	Opposite sides are parallel
Kite		2 sets of equal sides	1 set of opposite angles are equal	No parallel sides

Two parallelograms form the sides of the rocket. One big trapezium forms the main part of the rocket, a smaller trapezium forms the door and there's one rhombus for a window.

There are 4 triangles in the picture of a rocket but what type of triangles are they?

Again, the properties of some of the different triangles have been put into a table. Use the table to help you work out which triangles you can see in the picture of the rocket.

Name	Image	Sides	Angles
Right-angled Triangle		The sides do not have to be equal length	One of the angles is 90°
Equilateral Triangle		All sides are equal length	All angles are all 60°
Isosceles Triangle		Opposite sides are equal length	Two angles are equal

Three equilateral triangles form the tail of the rocket and one isosceles triangle forms its nose.

in the picture of the rocket, there are 3 equilateral triangles, 2 parallelograms, 2 trapeziums, 1 rhombus, and 1 isosceles triangle.

Make it easy!

Irregular quadrilaterals have no equal sides, no parallel sides and no equal angles.

Scalene triangles have no equal sides and no equal angles.

Now try this...

Which quadrilaterals cannot be seen in the picture of the rocket?

WHAT ARE THE NEW COORDINATES FOR THE ROCKET?

You are watching a Moon landing being streamed live. The rocket has not touched down in the correct place, as shown by the blue outline. Instead, it has landed 6 squares to the right and 2 squares down. What are the 5 new **coordinates** for where the rocket has landed?

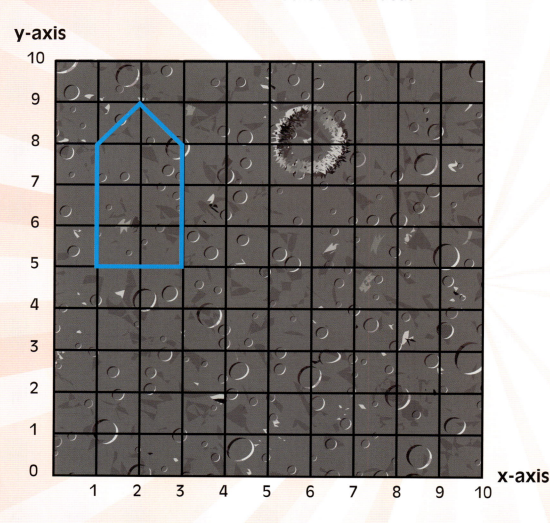

Start with the highest point of the rocket at the coordinates (2, 9). Count 6 squares to the right and then count 2 squares down and draw a dot on the new point. Repeat this process for each of the other corners of the rocket. Then join the dots.

Moving a shape in this way is called a **translation**. A translation is when a **2D shape** moves from one position to another without being flipped or rotated.

To describe a translation, you explain how many squares the 2D shape has moved to the left or right and how many squares the 2D shape has moved up or down.

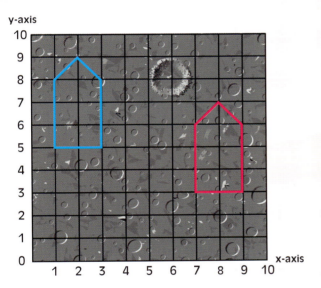

The rocket has moved 6 squares to the right and 2 squares down.

You can use coordinates to describe the exact position of the rocket. Remember when writing coordinates, you always write the number on the x-axis first.

The coordinates of the first rocket are: (2,9) (3,8) (3,5) (1,5) (1,8).

The new coordinates are:
(8,7) (9,6) (9,3) (7,3) (7,6).

Make it easy!

Can you remember your left from your right? Your left hand makes an L-shape if you stretch out your index finger and your thumb, but your right hand doesn't!

Trace the shape of the rocket and cut it out so you can physically move the whole rocket to make it easier.

Now try this...

What would the coordinates of the second rocket be if you moved it 3 squares to the left and 2 squares down?

WHICH PLANET HAS THE SHORTEST DAY?

The summer holiday starts in 2 days – that's only 48 hours! The time it takes for a planet to rotate on its **axis** once is called a day and some planets rotate faster than others. This means their days are shorter. Which planet has the shortest day? How long would you have to wait for the summer holiday to start if you were there?

These are the approximate times each planet in the solar system takes to make one rotation on its axis, or pass through one day.

Mercury takes 1,416 hours, Venus takes 5,832, Earth takes 24, Mars takes 25, Jupiter and Saturn take 10, Uranus takes 17 and Neptune takes 16.

Saturn
10 hours

Mercury
1,416 hours

Venus
5,832 hours

Earth
24 hours

Mars
25 hours

Jupiter
10 hours

Let's put this information in a table with the numbers in order, from largest to smallest, to make it easier to understand.

Planet	Approximate time taken to rotate once on its axis
Venus	5,832 hours
Mercury	1,416 hours
Mars	25 hours
Earth	24 hours
Uranus	17 hours
Neptune	16 hours
Jupiter	10 hours
Saturn	10 hours

Now it's easy to see Venus takes the greatest number of hours to do a complete rotation and Jupiter and Saturn take the fewest number of hours to do a complete rotation.

Now let's work out how long you'd have to wait for the summer holidays to start if you lived on Jupiter or Saturn. One day lasts ten hours on both of these planets so two days would last:

10 × 2 = 20

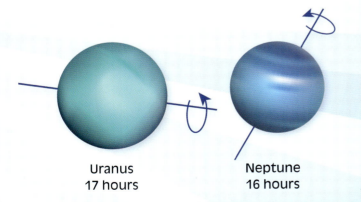

Uranus
17 hours

Neptune
16 hours

Both Jupiter and Saturn have the shortest days. On Earth you still have 2 days, or 48 hours, to wait until the summer holidays. But, if you were on Jupiter or Saturn, you'd only have to wait 20 hours until your holidays started.

Make it easy!

Placing information in **tables** and **graphs** makes it quicker and easier to understand.

Placing numbers in **columns** so their **place values** line up makes them easier to compare.

Now try this...

How much longer is a day on Mars compared to a day on Neptune?

GLOSSARY

2D shapes Flat shapes such as circles, and shapes with straight sides (polygons), such as triangles, quadrilaterals and pentagons.

Adjacent Next to.

Axis (1) One of the two lines framing a graph or chart. The horizontal line is the x-axis. The vertical line is the y-axis.(2) An imaginary line that a planet rotates around.

Bar chart A chart that displays data using rectangular bars of different heights.

Chunking Putting large numbers into smaller groups of the same size so they are easier to work with.

Coordinates Pairs of numbers that show the exact position on a map or graph. The first number shows how far along a point is on the x-axis. The second number shows how far up a point is on the y-axis.

Diameter A straight line going through the centre of a circle from edge to edge.

Digit A number symbol, e.g. 0, 1, 2, 3, 4, 5, 6, 7, 8, 9.

Estimate Round numbers up or down in sums to provide a good guess.

Frequency The number of times something happens within a set time or space (on a graph).

Inverse Opposite, e.g. addition is the inverse of subtraction, multiplication is the inverse of division, doubling is the inverse of halving.

Irregular Irregular shapes that have no edges or angles the same, e.g. a scalene triangle.

Numeral A symbol or a group of symbols representing a number, e.g. 176.

Operation The four mathematical operations are addition (+), subtraction (–), multiplication (×) and division (÷).

Quadrilaterals 2D shapes with four sides, including squares, rectangles, parallelograms, trapeziums, rhombuses and kites.

Radius The distance from the exact centre of a circle to its edge.

Rounding Adjusting numbers up or down to the nearest 10, 100 or 1,000.

Sequence A series of numbers with a particular pattern.

Table A chart displaying information in columns and rows.

Translation Moving a shape to a different position without changing it in any way.

Triangles 2D shapes with 3 sides and 3 angles. An equilateral triangle has 3 equal sides and 3 equal angles. A right-angled triangle has 3 sides and one of its angles will be exactly 90°. An isosceles triangle has 2 equal sides and 2 of its angles will be equal in size. A scalene triangle has no equal sides and no equal angles.

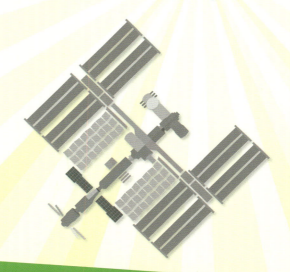

NOW TRY THIS... ANSWERS

Page 5

8,760 + 24 = 8,784

There are 8,784 hours in a leap year.

Page 7

Three thousand, three hundred and ninety-seven kilometres = 3,397 km

Page 9

Light takes 12 minutes and 40 seconds to travel from the Sun to Mars.

Page 11

103, 92, 81, 70, 59, 48, 37, 26, 15, 4

Page 13

7 months have three extra days each. 7 x 3 = 21

4 months have two extra days each. 4 x 2 = 8

21 + 8 = 29 (or 30 days in a leap year)

Page 15

25 – 20 = 5

5 more children recognised Cassiopeia than Orion.

Page 17

Nearest 10 = 49,530

Nearest 100 = 49, 500

Nearest 1,000 = 50,000

Page 19

8 ÷ 4 = 2

2 containers of space meals are required per person.

Page 21

60 + 30 = 90 minutes

Page 23

The New Horizons probe was 2 days, 17 hours and 53 minutes quicker than Apollo 16.

Page 25

There are no squares, rectangles or kites in the picture of a rocket.

Page 27

(5,5) (6,4) (6,1) (4,1) (4,4)

Page 29

25 – 16 = 9

A day on Mars is 9 hours longer than a day on Neptune.

First published in paperback in Great Britain in 2020 by Wayland

Produced for Wayland by Dynamo
Written by: Anita Loughrey

ISBN: 978 1 5263 0799 6

Wayland, an imprint of
Hachette Children's Group
Part of Hodder and Stoughton
Carmelite House
50 Victoria Embankment
London EC4Y 0DZ

An Hachette UK Company
www.hachette.co.uk
www.hachettechildrens.co.uk

Printed in China

MIX
Paper from
responsible sources
FSC® C104740
FSC
www.fsc.org

10 9 8 7 6 5 4 3 2 1

The website addresses (URLs) listed in this book were valid at the time of going to press. However, it is possible that the contents or addresses may have changed since the publication of this book. No responsibility for any such changes can be accepted by either the author or the Publisher.

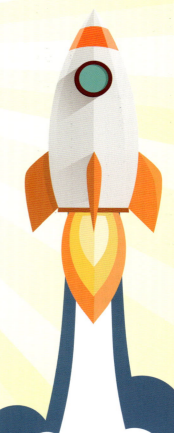